My Baby Is Hungry

Mi polluelo tiene hambre

At the White Sands National Monument in New Mexico the Red-tailed Hawk is at the top of the food chain. My Baby Is Hungry/Mi polluelo tiene hambre, will take the reader on an interesting journey of daily survival in the animal kingdom within its setting.

En el White Sands National Monument en Nuevo México el Halcón de Cola Roja es el primero en la cadena alimenticia. My Baby Is Hungry/Mi polluelo tiene hambre, llevará al lector a un interesante viaje de sobrevivencia cotidiana en el reino animal dentro de su entorno.

To my grandchildren Christian, Sydney and Magnolia with lots of love

A mis nietos Christian, Sydney y Magnolia con mucho amor

M.L.R.

The author acknowledges her husband, Guillermo, for accepting the invitation to narrate this story, and for his collaboration during the research part of this project. It is with gratitude that she also wants to thank her friend of many years, Diane Fahrner, for her constant support, encouragement and for assistance in editing the text and graphics for My Baby Is Hungry/Mi polluelo tiene hambre.

High Desert Productions

http://www.mariaretanabooks.com

Explore the world of the Red-tailed Hawk!

María L. Retana

Have you ever wondered how mama Red-tailed Hawk finds food for her baby?

¿Te has preguntado alguna vez cómo es que la mamá Halcón de Cola Roja encuentra la comida para su polluelo?

In this area, the Red-tailed Hawk sits at the very top of the food chain. Can you help me find a mother and her baby?

En este ámbito, el Halcón de Cola Roja es el primero en la cadena alimenticia.¿Me ayudarías a encontrar a una mamá y a su polluelo?

Did you say you will join me? Then come along and be part of the adventure.

¿Dijiste que me acompañarías? Entonces sígueme, y únete a la aventura.

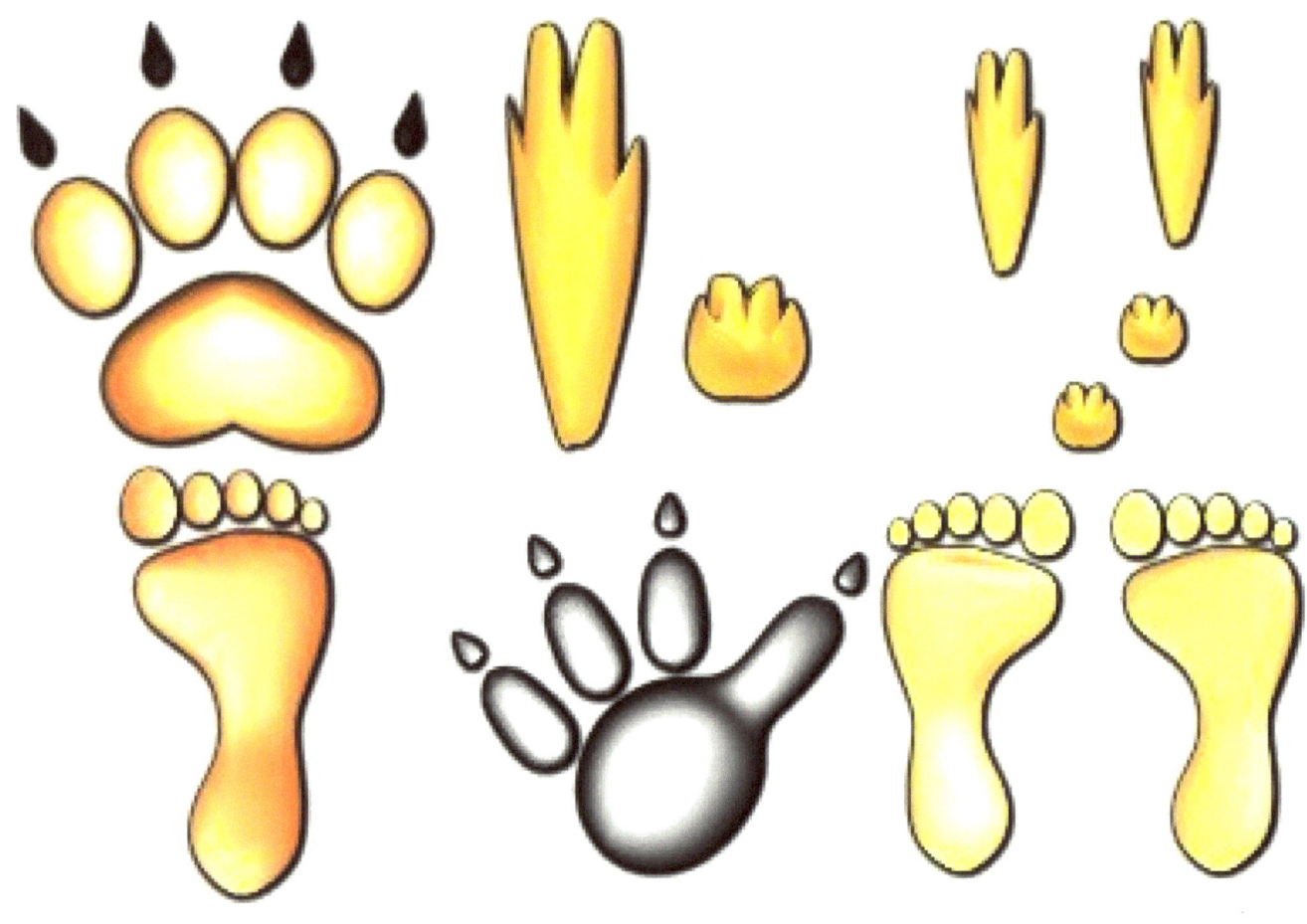

I see tracks! Are they human, or those of a polar bear? Let's follow the trail!

¡Veo huellas! ¿Son las de un ser humano, o las de un oso polar? ¡Sigámosle el rastro!

Oh, can you see what I see? It's a lizard right in front of its own tracks.

Oh, ¿ves lo que yo veo? Es un lagartijo enfrente de sus propias huellas.

He runs very fast. Can you find him in the photo?

Corre rápidamente. ¿Puedes encontrarlo en la foto?

Look! I see the tracks of another creature in the sand. Who do you think they belong to?

¡Mira! Veo huellas de otro animal en la arena. ¿De quién crees que son?

They are of a beautiful, colorful snake!

¡Son de una colorida y preciosa culebra!

Oh no the lizard will become lunch for the snake!

¡Oh no, el lagartijo será el almuerzo de la culebra!

And the snake will be lunch for...
Let's keep exploring! However, we will keep as close as possible to the snake. Remember, we want to know if she will become lunch for another desert creature at White Sands National Monument!

Y la culebra será el almuerzo de....
¡Sigamos averiguando! Mas sin embargo, nos mantendremos cerca de la culebra. ¡Recuerda, queremos saber si ella va a ser el almuerzo para otro animal del desierto en el White Sands National Monument!

I can see a bird in the distance, can you? Let's follow it!

En la distancia diviso un pájaro, ¿lo ves tú? ¡Sigámosle!

It is mama Red-tailed Hawk! While she is soaring I also hear her hoarse and rasping scream. She knows that snakes like to hide in the meadow to protect themselves from the desert heat and to digest their food.

¡Es mamá Halcón de Cola Roja! Mientras se abalanza también oigo su grito ronco y áspero. Ella sabe que a las culebras les gusta esconderse en la pradera para así protegerse del calor del desierto y para digerir su comida.

Little does the snake know, she will make a fine lunch for mother and baby.

Lo menos que se imagina la culebra es que hará un almuerzo delicioso para la mamá y su polluelo.

With her eyes fixed on the ground she attacks in a slow, controlled dive with legs outstretched.

Con los ojos fijos en el suelo ataca, enfrascándose lentamente con las patas extendidas.

Mama hawk uses her talons to pick up the snake and flies quickly to where her baby awaits.

Mamá halcón utiliza las garras para recoger la culebra y vuela rápidamente donde le espera su polluelo.

She patiently prepares her baby's lunch, tearing it apart for easy digestion. Does your mother cut your meat and veggies to bite-sized pieces for you?

Pacientemente prepara la comida de su polluelo, desmenuzándola para que pueda digerirla mejor.

¿Te corta tu mamá la carne y las verduras en pequeños trozos?

There, now baby is happy!

¡Ya el polluelo está satisfecho!

Thank you for joining me on this adventure. I hope you enjoyed learning about the food chain at White Sands National Monument.

Gracias por acompañarme en esta aventura. Espero que hayas gozado al aprender sobre la cadena alimenticia en el White Sands National Monument.

About the Author/Sobre la Autora

María Luisa Retana was born in Cuba. She received her B.A. in Spanish and Comparative Literature from the University of California, Riverside. She has worked extensively with children of all ages in scholastic and cultural events as well as in theater. She is the author of twelve published bilingual children's books and also a literary presenter for students, teachers, librarians, and parents. On December 2008 Mrs. Retana received her first literacy award given by the International Reading Association and the Cochise Area Council.

María Luisa Retana nació en Cuba. Se recibió con una Licenciatura en Literatura Española y Comparada de la Universidad de California en Riverside. Ha trabajado extensamente con niños de todas las edades en eventos escolares y culturales, e igualmente en teatro. Es la autora de doce libros bilingües para niños y es también presentadora literaria para estudiantes, maestros, bibliotecarios y padres. En diciembre del 2008 la Sra. Retana recibió su primer premio literario dado por The International Reading Association y por The Cochise Area Council.

Visit the authors website for more information about bilingual titles from High Desert Productions:
http://mariaretanabooks.com/

Dawn Till Dusk/De la aurora al crepúsculo

Grandma's Trunk / El baúl de Mamaíta

The Mystic Call / La llamada mística

Tanilí / Un Cuento Afrocubano
An Afrocuban Folktale

The Afternoon Snack / La Merienda

Born Into The Pack/ Nacer en la Manada

The Pig That is Not a Pig / El cerdo que no es cerdo

Free English only E-books from Website
http://mariaretanabooks.com/?page_id=3057

Where is Jazz?
A Child Says Goodbye to A Beloved Pet

Then A Sweet Trade Was Made
A Cuban Christmas Story